THE NEW WORLD ORDER

*In Drawing
and Sculpture*

1983-1993

Foreword and Comments by PATRICK OLIPHANT

Introduction by AUSTIN KIPLINGER

Exhibition Organized and Coordinated by
SUSAN CONWAY GALLERY IN WASHINGTON, D.C.

Published by ANDREWS AND MCMEEL, A Universal Press Syndicate Company
Kansas City

This exhibition was organized by Susan Conway Gallery, in conjunction with The Embassy of Austria, Washington, D.C. and is circulated by Susan Conway Gallery, Washington, D.C.

First Printing 1994

Library of Congress Cataloging-in-Publication Data

Oliphant, Pat, 1935-
    Oliphant : the new world order in drawing and sculpture, 1983-1993
/ foreword and comments by Patrick Oliphant ; introd. by Austin
Kiplinger ; exhibition organized and coordinated by Susan Conway
Gallery in Washington, D.C.
        p.   cm.
        Includes index.
        ISBN 0-8362-1755-1 : $12.95
        1. United States—Politics and government—1981-1989—Caricatures
and cartoons—Exhibition.   2. United States—Politics and
 government—1989-1993—Caricatures and cartoons—Exhibitions.
3. World politics—1985-1995—Caricatures and cartoons—Exhibitions.
4. American wit and humor, Pictorial—Exhibitions. 5. Sculpture,
American—Exhibitions. I. Susan Conway Gallery (Washington, D.C.)
II. Title.
E876.04524   1994   94-2147
909.82'8'0207—dc20   CIP

Photographers: Jeff McMillan
               Greg Staley
               Bill Auth

Designer: Stephen Kraft

Contents

Acknowledgments

The exhibition, *Oliphant: The New World Order in Drawing and Sculpture 1983-1993*, originated at the Embassy of Austria, Washington, D.C., and was toured by Susan Conway Gallery to Austria, Slovakia, Poland, the Czech Republic, and Hungary.

We are indebted to Austrian Cultural Attaches, Ferdinand Trauttmansdorff, who launched this endeavor in 1990, and his successor, Denise Quistorp-Rejc, whose enthusiasm and expertise helped at every turn. We thank her for her friendship, valuable collaboration and encouragement. Her support and that of Ambassador Hoess and Ambassador Tuerk of Austria, and the Austrian Cultural Institute have been invaluable.

For the occasion of this exhibition, Oliphant, as artist and author, has selected seventy-five political cartoon drawings from his body of work published internationally between 1983 and 1993. The comments written for the catalogue are his and are intended to recall for the reader the events of the day, putting each cartoon in context.

For 30 years, Patrick Oliphant has produced remarkable and insightful political cartoons which have both reflected and shaped public opinion in America. His accomplishments in sculpture, which he began in 1980, are equally evocative.

Alan Fern, Director of the National Portrait Gallery, Smithsonian Institution, has written about Oliphant:

> Few words suffice for him, as they did for Daumier, to underscore for the viewer what he is being invited to consider. The primary message is sent through the eloquent animation of the characters in the drawing, and through the rendition of the features of the recognizable principals. . . . an extraordinary display of portraiture as well as of political comment.

Mr. Trauttmansdorff believed that Oliphant's work, at once documents of American freedom of the press and documents of American art, would be particularly appreciated in the new Europe, having unique value as a bilateral cultural exchange. He suggested the theme of East-

West subjects, how Central and Eastern Europe are seen through American eyes.

At the same time, the role of the political cartoonist in American politics is revealed, giving a notion of the impact and importance of such visual commentary and its influence on public opinion in America.

Oliphant once wrote about the tradition of political cartooning:

Cartooning and caricature offer more than the photographic image or the fleeting electronic signal. A strong audience exists that needs to hold in the hand and contemplate a graphic distillation of the personality of the strutting popinjay on last night's news. This audience wants a visual rendering of immediacy and endurance that can be cut from the printed page and saved on the refrigerator, or if disliked, can be ripped from the page, have rude recommendations scrawled upon it, and mailed back to the artist. Such people, pro and con, possess awareness and opinion, and as such are to be blessed.

"Oliphant is an artist whose remarkable skill at caricature has deepened our understanding of recent Presidents and the modern Presidency," said Curator and scholar at the National Portrait Gallery, Wendy Wick Reaves. In this exhibition and publication, a full appreciation of Oliphant portrait portrayals and Wendy Reaves' appraisal of them are made possible.

We owe a special debt of gratitude to John McMeel of Andrews and McMeel, who made possible the publication of the catalogue, and to all his staff for their help, especially Tom Thornton, George Diggs, Bev Shiels and Dorothy O'Brien.

It is a pleasure to acknowledge our good friend and patron, and outstanding political and news commentator, Austin Kiplinger, Editor in Chief of America's foremost newsletter, *The Kiplinger Washington Letter,* for his generosity in writing the Introduction to the catalogue.

Special thanks are extended to Anne Kathryn Stokes, executive-assistant at Susan Conway Gallery, for her long hours tending to a myriad of details for the exhibition and tour; to our gallery intern, Sarah Moschler, for invaluable service, and to Pauline P. Conway for her assistance. In addition, we are grateful to photographers Jeff McMillan, Greg Staley and Bill Auth, and to Stephen Kraft for his handsome book design, and to Robyn Kennedy for her design and production of exhibition text, and for her helpfulness. And, as always, our deepest gratitude to one who is never seen but most key to our presentations and support system, Shelly Wischhusen, our chief installation designer.

SUSAN CORN CONWAY
Director
Susan Conway Gallery

Foreword

With the fall of the Soviet Empire, Europe and the world in general were thrown into a time of turbulent realignment. The old alliances on both sides of the Iron Curtain no longer had meaning: in fact, the Curtain itself ceased to exist.

As this new era began, citizens of the East and West fell upon the Berlin Wall with crowbars and sledge hammers. Entrepreneurs from the West moved into the East with dreams of influence and commerce, such once-fabled cities as Prague, Warsaw, Bratislava and Budapest glowed again with promise, new countries wrote themselves new constitutions, and all rushed headlong into the embrace of democracy. This, the world of the New Order, even sees NATO invite membership from the former members of the Warsaw Pact.

Such headiness is tempered by a darker side. We see now how the sudden lifting of repression created a vacuum and turned loose the ancient enmities of other eras, hatched the eggs of killer dinosaurs long extinct.

For political cartooning it has been the best of times and the worst of times.

The material itself is rich and endless. It delivers the ingredients of injustice, suffering and tragedy. It mines the depths and celebrates the heights of the human spirit. Nobody can completely grasp or cover it all. This is the stuff of history. Seventy or so drawings cannot, in any way, encompass an entire era, however short. But, perhaps, they can provide an outline, a flavor, an essence of opinion in a time of change and tumult. They should also remind us that leaders and leadership should always be considered with skepticism. That is the core of democracy.

With that in mind, I humbly offer for your consideration the following group of works.

PATRICK OLIPHANT

Introduction

Political cartooning has been a staple of a free press since the founding of representative government. It has drawn strength from artists and journalists the world over. Painters like Goya and engravers like Hogarth expressed their commentaries on society with brush and pen, and British cartoonists expressed their views of the "upstart American colonies" in no uncertain terms. Now cartooning is recognized as one of the most trenchant and influential voices of comment on the issues of the day.

We who are editors and reporters often envy the cartoonist for what seems like an inspired performance, even when we fully understand that a good cartoon does not spring magically from the head of Zeus without effort. We also understand that, since politics is an emotional experience, cartooning is at the heart of the political process. What is more important, we know that independent cartooning is a "litmus test" or final proof of freedom — freedom to express political views without official restraint.

In the early days of American democracy, cartoonists were merciless in their jabs at puffery, pretense, poltroons and demagoguery. They still are, and that is the everlasting value of the cartoonist's trade. Those of us who cannot draw are reduced to using words, but we know that they are sometimes a feeble substitute for the power of the picture.

So our hats are off to the cartoonists! Long may they live, and long may they defend the rights of the common man.

AUSTIN H. KIPLINGER

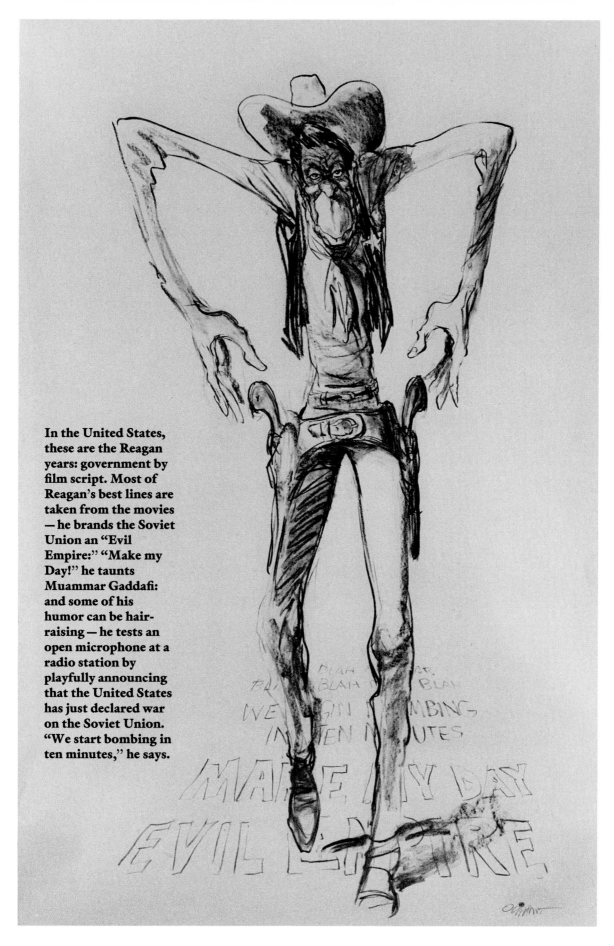

In the United States, these are the Reagan years: government by film script. Most of Reagan's best lines are taken from the movies — he brands the Soviet Union an "Evil Empire:" "Make my Day!" he taunts Muammar Gaddafi: and some of his humor can be hair-raising — he tests an open microphone at a radio station by playfully announcing that the United States has just declared war on the Soviet Union. "We start bombing in ten minutes," he says.

Forever the Cowboy, 1993, Charcoal on grey paper, 83 ½ x 53 inches
Courtesy of Susan Conway Gallery, Washington, D.C.

1. **Rockets** Ink/Brush March 16, 1983
Courtesy of Susan Conway Gallery, Washington, D.C.

A comfort for the
sanctimonious and the
self-righteous, and
God knows, we have
no shortage of either.

2. **Reagan and the Toad** Ink/Brush January 17, 1984
Courtesy of Susan Conway Gallery, Washington, D.C.

'..THEN, WHEN I KISS YOU, OLGA, YOU TURN FROM AN UGLY OLD TOAD INTO A NOT-TOO-BAD-LOOKING BROAD, AND WE LIVE MORE-OR-LESS HAPPILY EVER AFTER.'

At the beginning of an election year, Reagan seeks to temper his previous hard-line image and show U.S. flexibility on the eve of a major east-west conference on disarmament in Europe.

3. **Social Realism** Ink/Brush February 14, 1984
Courtesy of Susan Conway Gallery, Washington, D.C.

Under the old regime, the U.S.S.R. is grinding slowly to a halt.

4.   **Refuge**   Ink/Brush   June 4, 1985

Courtesy of Susan Conway Gallery, Washington, D.C.

Thirteen conservative U.S. Senators ask that President Reagan not comply with SALT II in light of continuing Soviet violations. Where is a rabbit to hide?

5. **The Basis of Understanding**   Pen/Ink/Brush   September 17, 1985
Courtesy of Susan Conway Gallery, Washington, D.C.

So Margaret Thatcher had said when Gorbachev visited Britain, but at this time a key Soviet Intelligence Agent defects to the U.K., Britain then expels 25 Soviets identified as spies. Moscow retaliates by expelling 25 Britons. When the dust settles, both countries have expelled 31 people.

6. **The Greenpeace Sinking**   Pen/Ink/Brush   September 23, 1985
Courtesy of Susan Conway Gallery, Washington, D.C.

Not every piece of news revolved around the failing Soviet Union. In New Zealand, the French sabotage and sink the Greenpeace trawler "Rainbow Warrior," which has been disrupting their nuclear tests in the South Pacific. The Mitterand government is subsequently charged with covering up the incident, which prompts this Nixon analogy.

7. **Summit**   Ink/Brush   October 2, 1985
Courtesy of Susan Conway Gallery, Washington, D.C.

Terrorism is now becoming the third world power.

8. **Take My Wife . . . Please!** Ink/Brush October 4, 1985
Courtesy of Susan Conway Gallery, Washington, D.C.

'SOME SLICKED-UP RUSSIAN TAPDANCER SAYS HE'S COME TO TAKE YOU AWAY FROM ALL THIS, MY DEAR.'

Russia borrows a few rubles for candy and flowers and goes off to court a married woman . . . not that her marriage is in great shape to begin with.

9. **The CIA Loses One**   Pen/Ink/Brush   November 6, 1985
Courtesy of Susan Conway Gallery, Washington, D.C.

SUDDENLY, INTUITIVELY, THE AWFUL REALIZATION HIT CIA AGENT, BUMWORTHY—HIS DINNER COMPANION, THE RUSSIAN DEFECTOR, WOULD NOT BE COMING BACK!

In Washington, a high ranking Soviet defector, Vitaly Yurchenko, is taken one cold November evening to a Georgetown restaurant by his Central Intelligence Agency handler. After a while, the defector excuses himself, goes back to the men's room, walks out a side door and strolls half a mile up Wisconsin Avenue to the Russian Embassy Compound, where he re-defects back to Russia. One must admit that international relations have their moments of humor, no matter who the players are . . .

10. **Three Defectors**   Ink/Brush/Black Pencil   November 7, 1985
Courtesy of Susan Conway Gallery, Washington, D.C.

... Provided, of
course, the players can
maintain that
humorous outlook.

11. **Sakharov** Pen/Ink/Brush December 10, 1985
Courtesy of Susan Conway Gallery, Washington, D.C.

HAPPY SAKHAROV DISSIDENTS IN SALT MINE PICNIC SCENE — *A KGB FILMS RELEASE*

The Soviets release videotapes showing the famous dissidents, 1975 Nobel Peace Prize winner Andrei Sakharov and his wife Yelena Bonner, hard at work enjoying themselves, in exile.

12. **The Boot from Gorby** Ink/Brush February 25, 1986
Courtesy of Susan Conway Gallery, Washington, D.C.

'PERSONALLY, I MUCH PREFERRED THE OLD LECTURE ABOUT THE INVINCIBLE INFALLIBILITY OF OUR SUPERIOR SYSTEM.'

This new agenda, declares Soviet leader Gorbachev, should not be regarded as a retreat from the principles of Socialism.

13. **The Faces of Perestroika**   Pen/Ink/Brush   March 6, 1986
Courtesy of Susan Conway Gallery, Washington, D.C.

**Gorbachev still
believes the exhausted
concept of Commu-
nism can be slapped
back into a usable
shape without
surrendering its
Socialist ideals . . . not
surprisingly, the
populace continues to
find solace in the wine
of the potato.**

14. **Chernobyl!** Ink/Brush April 29, 1986
Courtesy of Susan Conway Gallery, Washington, D.C.

' LET ME POINT OUT THAT IN THE UNITED STATES THIS HAPPENS ALL THE TIME!'

**The horror of
Chernobyl with, of
course, the inevitable
Soviet cover story.**

15. **Chernobyl, a Bad Note**   Ink/Brush   April 30, 1986
Courtesy of Susan Conway Gallery, Washington, D.C.

Soviet flatulence at
the European table.

16. **Ivan**   Ink/Brush   May 9, 1986
Courtesy of Susan Conway Gallery, Washington, D.C.

While in no way
mitigating the
egregious bungling at
Chernobyl, much of
the verbiage aimed at
the Soviets for that
disaster could be used
to describe NASA's
performance: the
space shuttle
"Challenger" explodes
shortly after
launching on January
28, 1986.

17. **Chernobyl Continues** Pen/Ink/Brush August 28, 1986
Courtesy of Susan Conway Gallery, Washington, D.C.

'OUR HEROIC TECHNICIANS HAVE MADE WHATEVER MINOR AND TRIVIAL ADJUSTMENTS WERE NECESSARY...'

Technicians are sent
into the Chernobyl
site to probe the cause
of the disaster. Brave
party officials
announce the status of
operations.

18. **Conservatives** Ink/Brush September 18, 1986
Courtesy of Susan Conway Gallery, Washington, D.C.

THE FAR RIGHT

'I'M DISGUSTED WITH REAGAN FOR CAVING IN TO THE RUSSIANS OVER DANILOFF
—BUT I **LOVE** THE WAY THE RUSSIANS TREAT THE PRESS!'

Nicholas Daniloff, Moscow correspondent for *U.S. News and World Report*, is arrested by the Soviet KGB for "engaging in acts of espionage."

19. **Daniloff** Ink/Brush September 22, 1986
Courtesy of Susan Conway Gallery, Washington, D.C.

This is viewed as
Soviet retaliation for
the U.S. arrest of
Gennadi Zakharov in
New York, on spying
charges. With a
Reagan-Gorbachev
summit to protect, the
U.S. works out a deal
to exchange Daniloff
for Zakharov.

20. **Elie Wiesel** Ink/Brush October 15, 1986
Courtesy of Susan Conway Gallery, Washington, D.C.

THE VIGIL — ELIE WIESEL, NOBEL PEACE PRIZE, 1986.

21. **Diplomatic Exchanges** Ink/Brush October 22, 1986
Courtesy of Susan Conway Gallery, Washington, D.C.

DIPLOMATIC EXCHANGES.

As an aftermath of this Daniloff affair, the U.S. and the Soviet Union trade diplomatic expulsions.

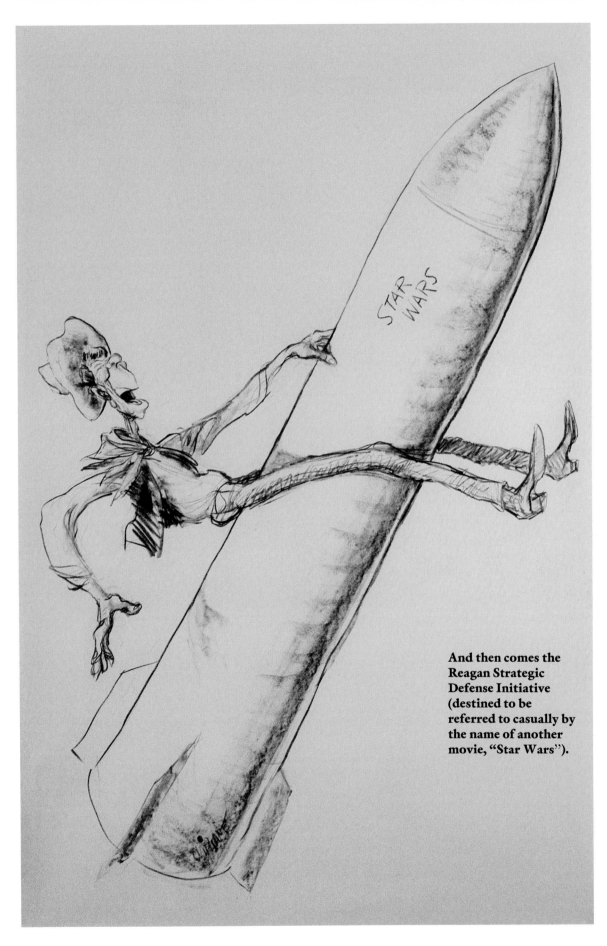

STAR
WARS

And then comes the Reagan Strategic Defense Initiative (destined to be referred to casually by the name of another movie, "Star Wars").

Forever the Cowboy II, 1993, Charcoal on grey paper, 80 x 52 inches
Courtesy of Susan Conway Gallery, Washington, D.C.

22. **Rex Reagan Space Hero**   Ink/Brush   January 15, 1987
Courtesy of Susan Conway Gallery, Washington, D.C.

Ronald Reagan never knew whether he belonged in the movies or the White House. Some of us thought he belonged in a comic strip. Here he is as Rex Reagan, Space Hero.

23. **Morning in the USSR** Pen/Ink/Brush February 11, 1987
Courtesy of Susan Conway Gallery, Washington, D.C.

Russian deeds juxtaposed with Reagan hyperbole is a mixture just too hard to resist.

24. **Kidnapped** Pen/Ink/Brush March 3, 1987
Courtesy of Susan Conway Gallery, Washington, D.C.

In a surprise move, Soviet leader Gorbachev calls for the U.S. and the USSR to eliminate medium-range nuclear missiles in Europe, this accord not to be tied to any other.

25. **People in Glasnosts**   Ink/Brush   March 30, 1987
Courtesy of Susan Conway Gallery, Washington, D.C.

PEOPLE IN GLASNOSTS...

Britain's Margaret Thatcher visits the USSR, confers with Gorbachev, and at a State banquet in her honor, spars with him on arms control and human rights.

26. **Klaus Barbie** Ink/Brush May 11, 1987
Courtesy of Susan Conway Gallery, Washington, D.C.

The trial of the infamous Klaus Barbie, who headed the German Gestapo in Lyon during World War II, opens in France. After the war, Barbie had worked for four years with U.S. Army, Counter Intelligence, which makes the U.S. position somewhat embarrassing. The French, similarly, are made nervous by possible public scrutiny of the activities of French collaborators during the German occupation.

27. **Exocet** Pen/Ink/Brush/Black Pencil May 20, 1987
Courtesy of Susan Conway Gallery, Washington, D.C.

Thirty-seven seamen are killed when the frigate, U.S.S. *Stark* is struck by a French Exocet missile fired by a French-built Iraqi warplane in the Persian Gulf.

28. **Baseball** Pen/Ink July 20, 1987
Courtesy of Susan Conway Gallery, Washington, D.C.

The Russians reveal one of the last of their Great Truths. Not only did they invent everything from the telephone and indoor plumbing to nuclear energy, radio, television and sliced bread. They also invented baseball.

29. **The Ron & Gorby Show** Pen/Ink/Brush/Adhesive Benday Tone December 1, 1987
Courtesy of Susan Conway Gallery, Washington, D.C.

Gorby (as he is fondly called everywhere outside Russia) is beginning to upstage The Great Communicator as a performing artist.

30. **The Verification Team** Ink/Brush May 11, 1988
Courtesy of Susan Conway Gallery, Washington, D.C.

A BEAUTY CONTEST: THE PRELIMINARIES.

**The I.N.F. Treaty will
eliminate U.S. and
USSR intermediate-
range missiles. Verifi-
cation comes later.**

31. **Mother Russia**   Pen/Ink/Brush   June 27, 1988
Courtesy of Susan Conway Gallery, Washington, D.C.

**Tough love from
Poppa Gorbachev.**

32. **All Wake Up!** Pen/Ink June 29, 1988
Courtesy of Susan Conway Gallery, Washington, D.C.

Somewhere in the Russian soul stirs the traces of entrepreneurialism. Some respond to it eagerly, some wonder what it is, some actively remain inactive.

33. **NASA** Pen/Ink/Brush September 28, 1988
Courtesy of Susan Conway Gallery, Washington, D.C.

With the launch of the shuttle "Discovery," the American Space Program revives after a despairing 32 month hiatus following the disastrous loss of the shuttle "Challenger."

34. **Circus** Pen/Ink/Brush November 29, 1988
Courtesy of Susan Conway Gallery, Washington, D.C.

`SIR, THE BEAR IS LOOSE...`

**Dissident conservative
bears.**

35. **Gorby in New York**   Ink/Brush   December 5, 1988
Courtesy of Susan Conway Gallery, Washington, D.C.

Soviet leader
Gorbachev, his wife
Raisa, and a large
party of Soviet
officials visit
Manhattan. His
purpose, as he states
it, is "to promote
greater dynamism in
the U.S.-Soviet
dialogue...." New
York is the world
capital of dynamic
dialogue.

36. **NATO** Pen/Ink/Brush December 12, 1988
Courtesy of Susan Conway Gallery, Washington, D.C.

**The U.S., having spent
half of its fortune on
the defense of Europe
against the Soviet
threat, asks
permission to retire.**

37. **Lands of Opportunity** Ink/Brush January 9, 1989
Courtesy of Susan Conway Gallery, Washington, D.C.

'PERHAPS VE COULD INTEREST YOU IN GLOBAL SUPREMACY THROUGH PHARMACEUTICAL INVESTMENT, JA?'

The global village at work. The U.S. lodges some 15 diplomatic complaints over foreign sales by West German companies of chemical weapons technology, missile technology and high-technology machine tools to such nations as Iran, Iraq, Syria, Pakistan and India.

38. **Exit Pollski** Pen/Ink/Brush/Adhesive Benday Tone March 24, 1989
Courtesy of Susan Conway Gallery, Washington, D.C.

'TELL YOU HOW I VOTED?? WHY, I THOUGHT THAT SORT OF INTRUSIVE MEDDLING WITH THE DEMOCRATIC PROCESS ONLY HAPPENED IN AMERICA!'

The Soviet Union held its first nationwide multi-candidate parliamentary elections since 1917.

39.   **The Berlin Wall Comes Down**   Pen/Ink/Brush/Black Pencil/Permanent White   November 10, 1989
Courtesy of Susan Conway Gallery, Washington, D.C.

'I JUST KEPT PECKING AT IT.'

**The Berlin Wall
comes down.**

40. **And Germany is Reunited** Pen/Ink/Brush December 12, 1989
Courtesy of Susan Conway Gallery, Washington, D.C.

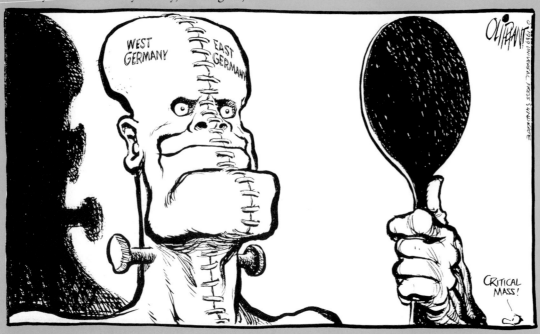

And Germany is
reunited.

41. **The Peace Prize** Pen/Ink/Brush October 15, 1989
Courtesy of Susan Conway Gallery, Washington, D.C.

Mikhail Gorbachev
wins the 1990 Nobel
Peace Prize. In the
West we all think it is
well-merited. At
home, not everyone is
elated.

48

42. **They Were Just Kidding** Pen/Ink/Brush November 21, 1989
Courtesy of Susan Conway Gallery, Washington, D.C.

'HOW D'YA LIKE THAT? MOSCOW SAYS TO FORGET ABOUT COMMUNISM — THEY WERE JUST KIDDING.'

43. **Urge to March**   Ink/Brush   February 9, 1990
Courtesy of Susan Conway Gallery, Washington, D.C.

**Germany reunited:
Beware the old
impulse.**

44. **Bootstraps** Ink/Brush July 22, 1991
Courtesy of Susan Conway Gallery, Washington, D.C.

'BOOTSTRAPS GORBACHEV... WHAT D'YOU THINK?'

45. **The Unravelling** Pen/Ink/Brush January 25, 1991
Courtesy of Susan Conway Gallery, Washington, D.C.

46. **Ballet** Pen/Ink/Brush/Adhesive Benday Tone August 20, 1991
Courtesy of Susan Conway Gallery, Washington, D.C.

Bolshoi in boots. The gentlemen here mentioned, Communist conservatives all, attempt to depose Mikhail Gorbachev while he is out of town.

47. **Nice Shot** Pen/Ink/Brush/Permanent White   August 22, 1991
Courtesy of Susan Conway Gallery, Washington, D.C.

NICE SHOT, MOTHER RUSSIA.

**Boris Yeltsin,
standing atop a tank,
leads the resistance to
the insurrection, and
the coup fails. Russia
stays a fledgling
Democracy.**

48. **Gorby and Yeltsin**   Pen/Ink/Brush   August 23, 1991
Courtesy of Susan Conway Gallery, Washington, D.C.

**Gorby returns, but
Yeltsin is the hero
of the moment.**

49. **Apparatchiks** Pen/Ink/Brush/Black Pencil August 30, 1991
Courtesy of Susan Conway Gallery, Washington, D.C.

'HEY, EVERYONE! REMEMBER HOW WE SAID WE'D LOVE TO GET OUR HANDS ON THOSE NASTY LITTLE COMMIE APPARATCHIK SUPERVISORS FROM THE HEROIC PEOPLES' SHIRT FACTORY...?

50. **McDonald's** Pen/Ink September 4, 1991

Courtesy of Susan Conway Gallery, Washington, D.C.

'ANOTHER HUNDRED MILLION BIG MACS, AND GET THE MESSAGE TO CONGRESS WE CAN'T DO ALL THIS ON OUR OWN!'

While the U.S. Congress drags its feet on financial aid to Russia, certain enterprising businesses are successfully working their own programs.

51. **Upstairs Downstairs** Pen/Ink/Brush December 10, 1991
Courtesy of Susan Conway Gallery, Washington, D.C.

Marital tension upstairs, nervous tension downstairs.

52. **We the People** Pen/Ink/Brush December 13, 1991
Courtesy of Susan Conway Gallery, Washington, D.C.

'WE, THE PEOPLE...'

Yeltsin has taken command. Gorbachev is more and more isolated.

53. **Peace** Pen/Ink/Brush/Permanent White December 24, 1991
Courtesy of Susan Conway Gallery, Washington, D.C.

And then, the USSR is no more. We cannot help but feel some gratitude to the man who started it all.

54. **The Unabled** Pen/Ink/Brush December 26, 1991
Courtesy of Susan Conway Gallery, Washington, D.C.

The Russians have
rejected Gorbachev:
The U.S., on the other
hand, still has Bush.
One has to wonder
which democracy is
the most successful.

55. **Shoes** Pen/Ink/Brush December 27, 1991
Courtesy of Susan Conway Gallery, Washington, D.C.

In the Gorbachev shoes.

56. **The Spectator** Pen/Ink February 11, 1992
Courtesy of Susan Conway Gallery, Washington, D.C.

Faced with great moments of decision, and seeing nothing of interest, Bush continues to pursue a course of masterly inaction.

57. **Bosnia** Pen/Ink/Brush July 1, 1992
Courtesy of Susan Conway Gallery, Washington, D.C.

'PLEASE, I NEED AN ABORTION!'

The Balkan States, no longer held together by Soviet suppression, return predictably to their intertribal habits of murder and mayhem.

Color Plates

Measurements are given in the following order: height, width, depth.

Clinton and Gore, 1993, Mixed media, 114 x 120 x 20 inches (over-all dimensions installed)
Courtesy of Susan Conway Gallery, Washington, D.C.

Clinton, 1993, Plaster, composite board, silkscreen, charcoal, and acrylic paint, 81 x 97 x 20 inches
Courtesy of Susan Conway Gallery, Washington, D.C.

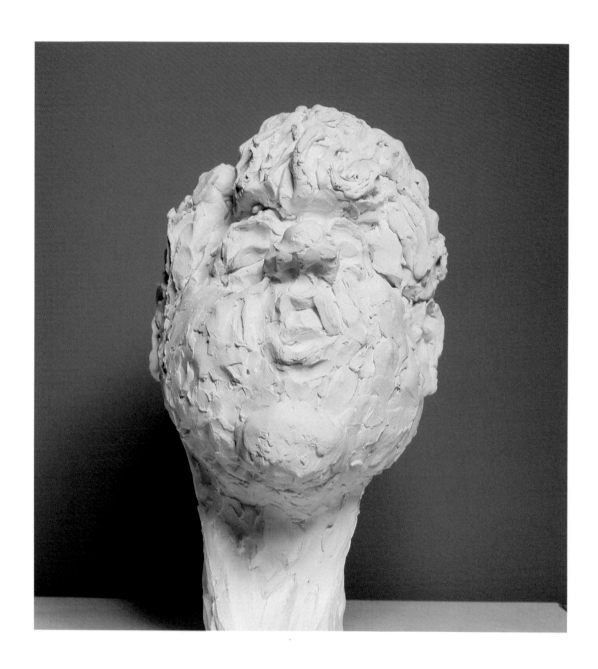

Clinton (detail)

Gore, 1993, Charcoal, acrylic paint, composite board, 72 x 10 x 1 inches
Courtesy of Susan Conway Gallery, Washington, D.C.

Gore (detail)

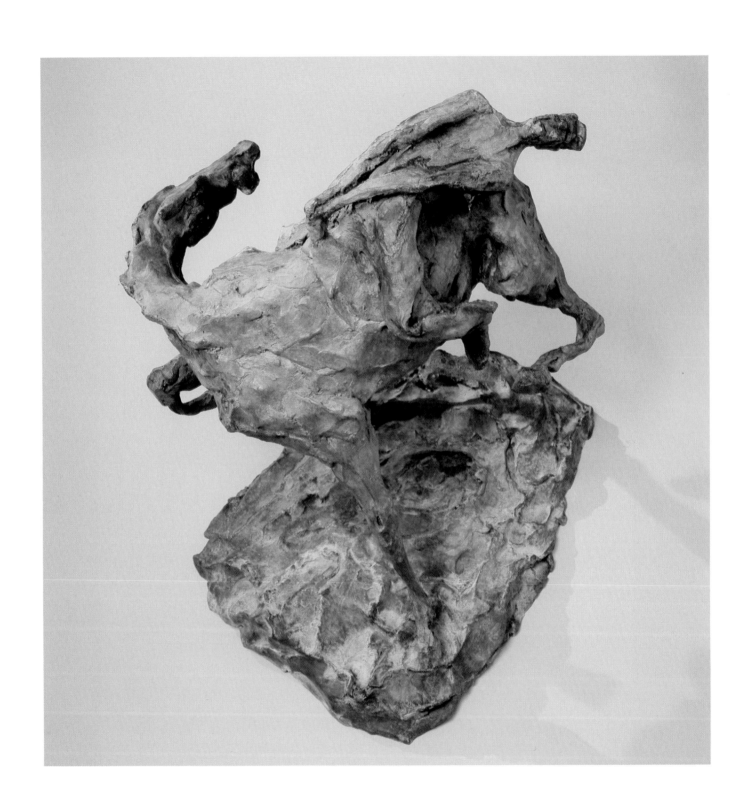

Reagan on Horseback, 1985, Bronze, 12 x 10¾ x 11½ inches, edition of 12
Courtesy of Susan Conway Gallery, Washington, D.C.

Bush of Arabia, 1991, Bronze, 9 x 2 ¾ x 4 ¼ inches, edition of 10
Courtesy of Susan Conway Gallery, Washington, D.C.

General Schwarzkopf, 1991, Bronze, 10 x 10 ¼ x 7 ½ inches, edition of 12
Courtesy of Susan Conway Gallery, Washington, D.C.

58. **Quagmire** Pen/Ink/Brush August 6, 1992
Courtesy of Susan Conway Gallery, Washington, D.C.

'PARDON ME – WHICH WAY TO THE QUAGMIRE?'

To each his own quagmire. What would life be without them?

59. **The View from Europe** Pen/Ink/Brush August 14, 1992
Courtesy of Susan Conway Gallery, Washington, D.C.

'CALL THE AMERICANS AND ASK WHAT THEY INTEND DOING ABOUT ALL THIS!'

If anyone should be interested in helping solve the Balkan problem, if such can ever be done, it must surely be the rest of Europe.

60. **Cafe Europe**   Pen/Ink   November 9, 1992
Courtesy of Susan Conway Gallery, Washington, D.C.

The European
Community nations
refuse to agree to U.S.
demands that it
further reduce
farming subsidies.
The U.S. counters
with a threat of 200%
tariffs on certain
goods from the E.C.

In Germany, the return of a bad dream.

In Somalia, as elsewhere, Europe dithers, discusses, and does little. On reflection, the U.S. would have done better to join the dithering.

63. **Kohl** Pen/Ink/Brush December 4, 1992
Courtesy of Susan Conway Gallery, Washington, D.C.

The government of Christian Democratic Chancellor Helmut Kohl has been criticized for months for not taking stronger action against Neo-Nazi violence.

64. **Yeltsin the Jogger**   Pen/Ink/Brush   December 16, 1992
Courtesy of Susan Conway Gallery, Washington, D.C.

Pursued by dissatisfaction and dissent, Boris Yeltsin fights his way through the volatile winter 1992 session of Congress. Gambling on his own popularity, he calls for a nation-wide referendum to be held in January 1993.

65. **The Menu**   Pen/Ink/Brush   December 18, 1992
Courtesy of Susan Conway Gallery, Washington, D.C.

66. The Serbs Next Door Pen/Ink/Brush/Permanent White December 26, 1992
Courtesy of Susan Conway Gallery, Washington, D.C.

U.S. President George Bush goes to war with Saddam Hussein when Hussein attacks Kuwait. The Kuwaitis, themselves renowned as rich, indolent cowards, are to be rescued by an amalgam of allies which includes a huge commitment of U.S. armed forces and technology. Many Americans cannot agree that the defense of Kuwait is worth the loss of one American life. Kuwait, however, has oil. The Russians later dismiss the following conflict, somewhat scornfully, as "target practice."

Bush of Arabia, 1993, Charcoal on grey paper, 85 x 47 inches
Courtesy of Susan Conway Gallery, Washington, D.C.

67. **Slow Learner**   Pen/Ink/Brush/Permanent White   January 15, 1993
Courtesy of Susan Conway Gallery, Washington, D.C.

SLOW LEARNER.

Either he is simply a slow learner or he is simply slow. Saddam Hussein continues to pursue military probes against Kuwait and invites U.N. reaction.

68. **Peace Plan for Bosnia** Ink/Brush/Pen February 3, 1993
Courtesy of Susan Conway Gallery, Washington, D.C.

'I DON'T SEE ANYTHING HERE WE CAN'T LIVE WITH.'

69. **Airdrop on Bosnia** Ink/Brush/Pen February 24, 1993
Courtesy of Susan Conway Gallery, Washington, D.C.

The U.S. begins air drops of food and medical supplies to Bosnia.

70. **Bosnia, Somalia and Russia**   Pen/Ink   March 17, 1993
Courtesy of Susan Conway Gallery, Washington, D.C.

Russia could, perhaps, be our most pressing priority.

71. **Nine Lives and Counting**   Pen/Ink   March 25, 1993
Courtesy of Susan Conway Gallery, Washington, D.C.

72. **Thank You for Not Interfering**   Ink/Brush/Pen   April 15, 1993
Courtesy of Susan Conway Gallery, Washington, D.C.

'THANK YOU FOR NOT INTERFERING.'

**The Bosnian slaughter
continues.**

73. **Clearinghouse Sweepstakes!**   Pen/Ink   April 19, 1993
Courtesy of Susan Conway Gallery, Washington, D.C.

Americans are used to receiving, in the mail, vain and elusive promises of great riches from sweepstakes which nobody ever seems to win. The U.S. Congress' promise of twenty-eight billion dollars seems reminiscent of this.

'OLGA! OLGA! IS RICH NATIONS' CLEARINGHOUSE SWEEPSTAKES! WE MAY HAVE ALREADY WON 28 BILLION DOLLARS!'

74. **Americans Welcome**   Ink/Brush/Pen   April 30, 1993
Courtesy of Susan Conway Gallery, Washington, D.C.

AMERICANS WELCOME.

75. **Guard Duty**   Pen/Ink   May 14, 1993
Courtesy of Susan Conway Gallery, Washington, D.C.

GUARD DUTY.

Checklist of Works

1. **Rockets**
Ink/Brush
March 16, 1983
Courtesy of Susan Conway Gallery,
Washington, D.C.

2. **Reagan and the Toad**
Ink/Brush
January 17, 1984
Courtesy of Susan Conway Gallery,
Washington, D.C.

3. **Social Realism**
Ink/Brush
February 14, 1984
Courtesy of Susan Conway Gallery,
Washington, D.C.

4. **Refuge**
Ink/Brush
June 4, 1985
Courtesy of Susan Conway Gallery,
Washington, D.C.

5. **The Basis of Understanding**
Pen/Ink/Brush
September 17, 1985
Courtesy of Susan Conway Gallery,
Washington, D.C.

6. **The Greenpeace Sinking**
Pen/Ink/Brush
September 23, 1985
Courtesy of Susan Conway Gallery,
Washington, D.C.

7. **Summit**
Ink/Brush
October 2, 1985
Courtesy of Susan Conway Gallery,
Washington, D.C.

8. **Take My Wife . . . Please!**
Ink/Brush
October 4, 1985
Courtesy of Susan Conway Gallery,
Washington, D.C.

9. **The CIA Loses One**
Pen/Ink/Brush
November 6, 1985
Courtesy of Susan Conway Gallery,
Washington, D.C.

10. **Three Defectors**
Ink/Brush/Black Pencil
November 7, 1985
Courtesy of Susan Conway Gallery,
Washington, D.C.

11. **Sakharov**
Pen/Ink/Brush
December 10, 1985
Courtesy of Susan Conway Gallery,
Washington, D.C.

12. **The Boot from Gorby**
Ink/Brush
February 25, 1986
Courtesy of Susan Conway Gallery,
Washington, D.C.

13. **The Faces of Perestroika**
Pen/Ink/Brush
March 6, 1986
Courtesy of Susan Conway Gallery,
Washington, D.C.

14. **Chernobyl!**
Ink/Brush
April 29, 1986
Courtesy of Susan Conway Gallery,
Washington, D.C.

15. **Chernobyl, a Bad Note**
Ink/Brush
April 30, 1986
Courtesy of Susan Conway Gallery,
Washington, D.C.

16. **Ivan**
Ink/Brush
May 9, 1986
Courtesy of Susan Conway Gallery,
Washington, D.C.

17. **Chernobyl Continues**
Pen/Ink/Brush
August 28, 1986
Courtesy of Susan Conway Gallery,
Washington, D.C.

18. **Conservatives**
Ink/Brush
September 18, 1986
Courtesy of Susan Conway Gallery,
Washington, D.C.

19. **Daniloff**
Ink/Brush
September 22, 1986
Courtesy of Susan Conway Gallery,
Washington, D.C.

20. **Elie Wiesel**
Ink/Brush
October 15, 1986
Courtesy of Susan Conway Gallery,
Washington, D.C.

21. **Diplomatic Exchanges**
Ink/Brush
October 22, 1986
Courtesy of Susan Conway Gallery,
Washington, D.C.

22. **Rex Reagan Space Hero**
Ink/Brush
January 15, 1987
Courtesy of Susan Conway Gallery,
Washington, D.C.

23. **Morning in the USSR**
Pen/Ink/Brush
February 11, 1987
Courtesy of Susan Conway Gallery,
Washington, D.C.

24. **Kidnapped**
Pen/Ink/Brush
March 3, 1987
Courtesy of Susan Conway Gallery,
Washington, D.C.

25. **People in Glasnosts**
Ink/Brush
March 30, 1987
Courtesy of Susan Conway Gallery,
Washington, D.C.

26. **Klaus Barbie**
Ink/Brush
May 11, 1987
Courtesy of Susan Conway Gallery,
Washington, D.C.

27. **Exocet**
Pen/Ink/Brush/Black Pencil
May 20, 1987
Courtesy of Susan Conway Gallery,
Washington, D.C.

28. **Baseball**
Pen/Ink
July 20, 1987
Courtesy of Susan Conway Gallery,
Washington, D.C.

29. **The Ron & Gorby Show**
Pen/Ink/Brush/Adhesive Benday Tone
December 1, 1987
Courtesy of Susan Conway Gallery,
Washington, D.C.

30. **The Verification Team**
Ink/Brush
May 11, 1988
Courtesy of Susan Conway Gallery,
Washington, D.C.

31. **Mother Russia**
Pen/Ink/Brush
June 27, 1988
Courtesy of Susan Conway Gallery,
Washington, D.C.

32. **All Wake Up!**
Pen/Ink
June 29, 1988
Courtesy of Susan Conway Gallery,
Washington, D.C.

33. **NASA**
Pen/Ink/Brush
September 28, 1988
Courtesy of Susan Conway Gallery,
Washington, D.C.

34. **Circus**
Pen/Ink/Brush
November 29, 1988
Courtesy of Susan Conway Gallery,
Washington, D.C.

35. **Gorby in New York**
Ink/Brush
December 5, 1988
Courtesy of Susan Conway Gallery,
Washington, D.C.

36. **NATO**
Pen/Ink/Brush
December 12, 1988
Courtesy of Susan Conway Gallery,
Washington, D.C.

37. **Lands of Opportunity**
Ink/Brush
January 9, 1989
Courtesy of Susan Conway Gallery,
Washington, D.C.

38. **Exit Pollski**
Pen/Ink/Brush/Adhesive Benday Tone
March 24, 1989
Courtesy of Susan Conway Gallery,
Washington, D.C.

39. **The Berlin Wall Comes Down**
Pen/Ink/Brush/Black Pencil/
Permanent White
November 10, 1989
Courtesy of Susan Conway Gallery,
Washington, D.C.

40. **And Germany is Reunited**
Pen/Ink/Brush
December 12, 1989
Courtesy of Susan Conway Gallery,
Washington, D.C.

41. **The Peace Prize**
Pen/Ink/Brush
October 15, 1989
Courtesy of Susan Conway Gallery,
Washington, D.C.

42. **They Were Just Kidding**
Pen/Ink/Brush
November 21, 1989
Courtesy of Susan Conway Gallery,
Washington, D.C.

43. **Urge to March**
Ink/Brush
February 9, 1990
Courtesy of Susan Conway Gallery,
Washington, D.C.

44. **Bootstraps**
Ink/Brush
July 22, 1991
Courtesy of Susan Conway Gallery,
Washington, D.C.

45. **The Unravelling**
Pen/Ink/Brush
January 25, 1991
Courtesy of Susan Conway Gallery,
Washington, D.C.

46. **Ballet**
Pen/Ink/Brush/Adhesive Benday Tone
August 20, 1991
Courtesy of Susan Conway Gallery,
Washington, D.C.

47. **Nice Shot**
Pen/Ink/Brush/Permanent White
August 22, 1991
Courtesy of Susan Conway Gallery,
Washington, D.C.

48. **Gorby and Yeltsin**
Pen/Ink/Brush
August 23, 1991
Courtesy of Susan Conway Gallery,
Washington, D.C.

49. **Apparatchiks**
Pen/Ink/Brush/Black Pencil
August 30, 1991
Courtesy of Susan Conway Gallery,
Washington, D.C.

50. **McDonald's**
Pen/Ink
September 4, 1991
Courtesy of Susan Conway Gallery,
Washington, D.C.

51. **Upstairs Downstairs**
Pen/Ink/Brush
December 10, 1991
Courtesy of Susan Conway Gallery,
Washington, D.C.

52. **We the People**
Pen/Ink/Brush
December 13, 1991
Courtesy of Susan Conway Gallery,
Washington, D.C.

53. **Peace**
Pen/Ink/Brush/Permanent White
December 24, 1991
Courtesy of Susan Conway Gallery,
Washington, D.C.

54. **The Unabled**
Pen/Ink/Brush
December 26, 1991
Courtesy of Susan Conway Gallery,
Washington, D.C.

55. **Shoes**
Pen/Ink/Brush
December 27, 1991
Courtesy of Susan Conway Gallery,
Washington, D.C.

56. **The Spectator**
Pen/Ink
February 11, 1992
Courtesy of Susan Conway Gallery,
Washington, D.C.

57. **Bosnia**
Pen/Ink/Brush
July 1, 1992
Courtesy of Susan Conway Gallery,
Washington, D.C.

58. **Quagmire**
Pen/Ink/Brush
August 6, 1992
Courtesy of Susan Conway Gallery,
Washington, D.C.

59. **The View from Europe**
Pen/Ink/Brush
August 14, 1992
Courtesy of Susan Conway Gallery,
Washington, D.C.

60. **Cafe Europe**
Pen/Ink
November 9, 1992
Courtesy of Susan Conway Gallery,
Washington, D.C.

61. **Deutschland**
Pen/Ink
November 12, 1992
Courtesy of Susan Conway Gallery,
Washington, D.C.

62. **Somalia**
Pen/Ink/Brush
December 2, 1992
Courtesy of Susan Conway Gallery,
Washington, D.C.

63. **Kohl**
Pen/Ink/Brush
December 4, 1992
Courtesy of Susan Conway Gallery,
Washington, D.C.

64. **Yeltsin the Jogger**
Pen/Ink/Brush
December 16, 1992
Courtesy of Susan Conway Gallery,
Washington, D.C.

65. **The Menu**
Pen/Ink/Brush
December 18, 1992
Courtesy of Susan Conway Gallery,
Washington, D.C.

66. **The Serbs Next Door**
Pen/Ink/Brush/Permanent White
December 26, 1992
Courtesy of Susan Conway Gallery,
Washington, D.C.

67. **Slow Learner**
Pen/Ink/Brush/Permanent White
January 15, 1993
Courtesy of Susan Conway Gallery,
Washington, D.C.

68. **Peace Plan for Bosnia**
Ink/Brush/Pen
February 3, 1993
Courtesy of Susan Conway Gallery,
Washington, D.C.

69. **Airdrop on Bosnia**
Ink/Brush/Pen
February 24, 1993
Courtesy of Susan Conway Gallery,
Washington, D.C.

70. **Bosnia, Somalia and Russia**
Pen/Ink
March 17, 1993
Courtesy of Susan Conway Gallery,
Washington, D.C.

71. **Nine Lives and Counting**
Pen/Ink
March 25, 1993
Courtesy of Susan Conway Gallery,
Washington, D.C.

72. **Thank You for Not Interfering**
Ink/Brush/Pen
April 15, 1993
Courtesy of Susan Conway Gallery,
Washington, D.C.

73. **Clearinghouse Sweepstakes!**
Pen/Ink
April 19, 1993
Courtesy of Susan Conway Gallery,
Washington, D.C.

74. **Americans Welcome**
Ink/Brush/Pen
April 30, 1993
Courtesy of Susan Conway Gallery,
Washington, D.C.

75. **Guard Duty**
Pen/Ink
May 14, 1993
Courtesy of Susan Conway Gallery,
Washington, D.C.

Index